Managerial Implications of the Tabuk Campaign

Prof Javed Iqbal Saani
PhD, MBA (MIS), MBA (Finance), BBA

Intellectual Capital Enterprise
Limited, London

Copyright © 2019 Prof Javed Iqbal Saani

All rights reserved.

No reproduction of the book in any form such as electronic, photocopying, scanning, recording or otherwise. It also includes storing for retrieval purpose or transmitting through electronic media i.e. email. Prior written permission of the publisher may require doing any of the above under the relevant act that follows the Copyright, Design, and Patent Act 1988.

Authors and the publisher are not responsible for any damage caused by the application/use of the concepts, techniques, instruction, or actions.

The authors and publisher refuse any implied warranties or related matters.

ISBN: 9781795295796

Published by Intellectual Capital Enterprise Limited
ICE Kemp House, 152-160 City Road
London, EC1 V2N
Printed in England

CONTENTS

About the author	v
Dedication	xv
Acknowledgment	xvii
Preface	xix

1 THE EXPEDITION — 1

Introduction	1
Background	2
Preparations	4
The expedition and its Impacts	6

2 MANAGEMENT OF HUMAN RESOURCE — 9

Introduction	9
What is Human resource management?	9
Staffing	10
Resourcing/compensation and benefits	12
Defining/designing work	13
Motivation	15
Managing discipline	19

3 FINANCIAL MANAGEMENT — 21

Introduction	21
What is fiscal management?	22

Acquisition of resources	23
Utilisation of resources	24
Reservation of resources	25
4 STRATEGIC MANGEMENT	**27**
Introduction	27
Nature of strategic management?	27
Background	28
Strategic intent	30
Planning the expedition	30
Implementation	33
Evaluation	36
5 INFORMATION MANAGEMENT	**39**
Introduction	39
Information management	39
Written communication	41
Dissemination of information	43
Key points	44
Bibliography	*47*
Index	*55*
Other books by the author (s)	*59*
Notes	*89*

About the author

Javed Iqbal was brought up in Rawalakot (AJ&K). He received his Ph.D. from the University of Salford and an MBA (Information Management) from the University of Hull. Previously Dr. Iqbal received a BBA and an MBA (in Finance) from the University of AJ&K both with distinction.

Professor Iqbal joined IQRA University Islamabad campus as an associate professor in 2006. He became the head of Department of Technology Management in International Islamic University Islamabad (IIUI) in 2012. Dr. Iqbal joined AKU (AJ&K) as a professor in 2015 and has been appointed as a Dean Faculty of Management Sciences. He is associated with London School of Commerce (LSC) these days. His article titled "Learning from a Doctoral Research Project: Structure and Content of a Research Proposal" has been ranked by the Deakin University of Australia as the best piece of research for doctoral students. This  research paper is widely used and referred to all over the world. Dr. Javed Iqbal has been nominated by an international organization for the Award of Distinguished Scientist for his research contribution. Professor Iqbal has published twenty-two research articles and twenty-three books so far. He has developed an interest in Islamic Leadership Style recently. Professor Iqbal has published in many International Journals His books on various subjects are available on Amazon, details are at the end of the book.

Value of knowledge

Say (to them, O Muhammad): Are those who know equal with those who know not? But only men of understanding will pay heed. [Az-Zumar: 9]

Value of knowledge I

Anas (May Allah be pleased with him) reported: The Messenger of Allah (ﷺ) said, "He who goes forth in search of knowledge is considered as struggling in the Cause of Allah until he returns." [At-Tirmidhi].

Value of Knowledge II

Abu'd-Darda' (رضي الله عنه) said, "I heard the Messenger of Allah, may Allah bless him and grant him peace, say,

1. 'Allah will make the path to the Garden easy for anyone who travels a path in search of knowledge.

2. Angels spread their wings for the seeker of knowledge out of pleasure for what he is doing.

3. Everyone in the heavens and everyone in the earth asks forgiveness for a man of knowledge, even the fish in the water.

4. The superiority of the man of knowledge to the man of worship is like the superiority of the moon to all the planets.

5. The men of knowledge are the heirs of the Prophet (ﷺ)'s (ﷺ).

6. The Prophet (ﷺ)'s (ﷺ) bequeath neither dinar nor dirham; they bequeath knowledge. Whoever takes it has taken an ample portion.'"

[Abu Dawud and at-Tirmidhi; Riyadh us Salihin, Hadith 1388, p. 211]

Qualities of good leader/manager

It was by the mercy of God that you were lenient with them (O Muhammad), for if you had been severe and hard-hearted, they would have forsaken you. So, pardon them and ask (God's) forgiveness for them and consult with them upon the conduct of affairs. [Al-e-Imran: 159]

Qualities of good leader/manager 1

Hadhrat Ibn 'Umar (Radhi Allah anho) reports that Rasulullah (Sallallaho alaihe wasallam) said "Three persons are such as will have no fear of the horrors of the Day of Judgement, nor they will be required to render an account. They will stroll merrily on mounds of musk until the people are relieved of rendering their account. One is a person who learned the Qur'an, merely seeking Allah's pleasure and therewith leads people in salaat in a manner that they are pleased with him; the second person is the one who invites men to salaat for the pleasure of Allah alone. <u>The third person is the one who has fair dealings between him and his master, as well as between himself and his subordinates</u>" [Quoted by Al-Tibrani in Al-Majam Al-Slaasa; Fazail-e-Amaal, Virtues of the Holy Qur'an, Hadith 36]

Qualities of good leader/manager II

Abdullah ibn-e-'Umar Radiyallahu 'anhuma narrates that a person came to Nabi and asked: O Rasulullah (ﷺ)! How many times may I forgive my servant? Nabi remained silent. <u>The man asked again: O Rasulullah (ﷺ)! How many times may I forgive my servant? He replied: Everyday seventy times.</u> (Tirmidhi) Note: In Arabic, the figure 'seventy' is used to express too many in number. [Muntakhib Ahadith, p. 415]

Allah, the Exalted

In the name of Allah, the Beneficent, the Merciful.

1. All that is in the heavens and the earth glorifieth Allah; and He is the Mighty, the Wise. 2. His is the Sovereignty of the heavens and the earth; He quickeneth and He giveth death, and He can do all things. 3. He is the First and the Last, and the Outward and the Inward, and He is Knower of all things. 4. He is Who created the heavens and the earth in six Days; then He mounted the Throne. He knoweth all that entereth the earth and all that emergeth therefrom and all that cometh down from the sky and all that ascendeth therein, and He is with you wheresoever ye may be. And Allah is Seer of what ye do. 5. His is the Sovereignty of the heavens and the earth, and unto Allah (all) things are brought back. 6. He causeth the night to pass into the day, and He causeth the day to pass into the night, and He is the knower of all that is in the breasts.

Dedication

To my parents who invested heavily for our education and remained engaged in prayers for our success and wellbeing.

Acknowledgment

Special gratitude is due to all those who helped me to compile the work. I am also obliged to my family who spared me to embark on the project. They also provide valuable information which enriched the contents of this effort. May Allah (SWT) reward them for their contribution? Ameen!

Preface

All prayers to Allah, the exalted, slat wa slam to all the Prophet (ﷺ)s (AS) especially upon the last (ﷺ), mercy and blessings upon his noble companions. May Allah (SWT) bestow upon his forgiveness to the entire ummah and ummah of all the Prophet (ﷺ)s (AS). And all those who received the right guidance.

The battle of Tabuk is unique because the Prophet (ﷺ) had travelled hundreds of miles away from Madinah to encounter one of the superpowers of the time but the enemy did not dare to challenge the Muslims. It was a victory without any fight which has created the long-term impacts on the area and all over the world.

The book has been divided into four chapters. The first one deals with the summary of the events. The second one is discussing the strategic management. Strategic management is dealing with the long-term impacts of any event or product. Therefore, the focus of this chapter is to discuss various aspects of the topic: the strategic intent, the formulation of strategy and implementation of it to achieve the long-term objectives. The next chapter is dealing with human resource management which is associated with the previous chapter. It discusses the acquisition, training, and retention of employees. It also includes motivation and reward system. Information management is one of the crucial areas in business these days and it was also especially important for managing battles. So, the chapter is dealing with the process of managing information during the event. We understand that it was a successful journey which partly depended upon the quality of information management. It concerned with acquisition of information, preservation of information, and making informed decision according to the intelligence provided by the relevant people. The next chapter is discussing the financial aspects of the event. The purpose of fiscal management is to acquire financial resources and apply them for financing different activities. To keep reserve of remaining resources which could be utilised in the future. The concluding chapter is reserved for some miscellaneous aspects.

I pray to Allah, the Exalted, to accept the humble effort and make it a source of forgiveness for me and the entire ummah. May it be a source of guidance for readers. Ameen!

Suggestions are welcome so that they may be incorporated in the future editions.

Prof Javed Iqbal Saani, Ph. D
Manchester January 28, 2019

1 THE EXPEDITION

Introduction

We understand that this is one of the battles which took 50 days to complete. Whenever we study a case study, we tried to implicate the managerial implications which can be learnt from such case studies. The contemporary managers can use the learning for managing their organisations. We aim to identify the fact that the Prophet (ﷺ) had applied the managerial techniques such as Human Resource Management (HRM) long time ago which contemporary managers are applying these days. It means that the Prophet (ﷺ) was one of the efficient managers who has utilised the resources of his organisation effectively and efficiently. And this is what the purpose of a manager is.

One way to judge the efficiency of a manager is to measure his productivity. It is "the efficient use of resources, labour, capital, land, materials, energy, information, in the production of various goods and services. Higher productivity means accomplishing more with the same number of resources or achieving higher output in terms of volume and quality from the same input."¹ It is the ratio of output to inputs. It is also known as the productivity in the contemporary management concepts; the productivity of the Prophet (ﷺ) and his followers was extremely high. If we measure the productivity in terms of the participants in the battles. We can say that in the first battle there were only 313 people while in the second battle the number increased to 700; in the third battle the number increase to 3000 and it boosted to 10000 (in conquering of Makkah). The participants of Hunain were 12,000. |The final expedition of the Prophet (ﷺ) involved 30,000 people so it was one of the major expeditions.

Background
The enmity emerged with Romans when they martyred the Muslim envoy Hazrat Haris bin Umair Azri (RA). In response, the Prophet (ﷺ) had sent a small contingent under the command of Zaid bin Harsa (RA) who fought with the battle of Mota. However, the strength of the opponents was still considerable.

The immediate reason of this battle was the threat of Romans to invade Madinah. Also, after the defeat of Quraysh most of the Arab tribes where in favour of the Muslims. New tribes were entering in the fold of Islam and

---

¹http://www.employment.gov.sc/what-is-productivity

other tribes were considering embracing the new religion. Mubarikpuri states the worry of Byzantine Empire,

> Caesar — who could neither ignore the great benefit the Mu'tah Battle had brought to Muslims, nor could he disregard the Arab tribes' expectations of independence, and their hopes of getting free from his influence and reign, nor he could ignore their alliance to the Muslims — realizing all that, Caesar was aware of the progressive danger threatening his borders, especially Ash-Sham-fronts which were neighbouring Arab lands. So, he concluded that demolition of the Muslims power had grown an urgent necessity. This decision of his should be achieved before the Muslims become too powerful to conquer and raise troubles and unrest in the adjacent Arab territories.[2]

To materialise these ambitions the Byzantines decided to initiate a decisive step to neutralise Muslim power. They gathered a large army with the help of their Arab confederates. At one point the enemy gathered 40,000 strong army and gathered in Belqa. It ignited the hopes of hypocrites of Madinah and surroundings. They wanted to eliminate Muslims as soon as possible at any cost. Therefore, they had constructed a separate place of worship so that they can conspire in privacy. It provided them a base camp for

---

[2] P. 579.

planning their malicious aspires. They were so much dare that they had invited the Prophet (ﷺ) to lead a prayer in the new place. The Prophet (ﷺ) postponed it till his return from the campaign.

The purpose of the Battle was to show Romans and others that Muslims were now a real military power in the area. The Battle would have completed the influence of Muslims in Arab lands; it was also a decent effort to control the hypocrites and others indeed.

Preparations

The Prophet (ﷺ) had recruited the companion from Medina, Arab tribes, and Makkah. In addition to the manpower, the Prophet (ﷺ) had contributed a lot of money and resources from Muslims to finance the army. He had appointed a deputy (Governor of Madinah) and deputed Ali (RA) for looking after his family. A vast number of people gathered to accompany the Prophet (ﷺ).

On ground, the physical circumstances were very odd. It was extremely hot, people were threatened with famine and poverty, mounts were limited, the crops were ready and the journey was long. It restricted people to go immediately for the campaign.

Nevertheless, the Prophet (ﷺ) had taken a decisive decision to go out at all costs. He knew that the invasion of Byzantines would create bad image of Muslims, they could lose the advantages of the previous conquests. The possibility of revival of idolaters could not be ruled out.

As a result, the Prophet (ﷺ) had announced the expedition. He invited people of Makkah, the confederate tribes, and the inhabitants of Madinah. He inspired people for fighting for the cause of Allah (SWT) and motivated them for spending in the path of Almighty. The companions had contributed generously but there was lack of resources due to the substantial number of participants. Many willing to join the campaign could not accompany the troops because of unavailability of mounts. Usman (RA), Abdurrehman bin Ouff (RA), Abu Bakr (RA), Umer (RA), Abbass (RA), Talha (RA), Saad bin Ubaidhah (RA), Muhammad bin Musalmah (RA), Asim bin Addi (RA) were the prominent contributors. Women also took part enthusiastically in the collection.

Passionate tribes and people gathered quickly on the call of the Prophet (ﷺ). Lings described the movements.

> When all the Bedouin contingents had arrived, the army was thirty thousand strong, with ten thousand horses. A camp was made outside the town, and Abu Bakr was put in charge of it until, when all was ready for the march, the

Prophet (ﷺ) himself rode forth and took command.³

The expedition and its Impacts
It took him fifteen days to reach the destination. The Romans could not dare to face Muslims.
The Prophet (ﷺ) stayed twenty days in the area and send many expeditions for conquering adjunct areas. Khalidh bin Waleedh (RA) was sent to Dhuma-tul_Jandhal with more than four hundred soldiers. The leader of Dhuma offered a large amount of booty and agreed to pay protection tax. The chiefs of Eilah, Herbah, and Azrah also followed him. The Prophet (ﷺ) had written a truce for them,

The Prophet (ﷺ) returned to Madinah and managed the Muslims who could not join him. Three true Muslims were reprimanded for fifty days because the Prophet (ﷺ) stayed out on their expedition for fifty days. Therefore, their social boycott was for the same period.

The battle created positive effects on the other tribes. Most of them embraced Islam within a brief period of two years prior to the death of the Prophet (ﷺ). The people of Arab started to support Muslims who were under the influence of Romans. It helped Muslim to concentrate on learning and teaching and expanding the

---
³ P. 318.

message of Islam to the remaining areas of the Arab lands.

2 MANAGEMENT OF HUMAN RESOURCE

Introduction
The purpose of this chapter is to explore the human resource management (HRM) out of case study. The topic has been chosen because there were many people participated in the expedition which means that it involves the management of people including selection, motivating, and resourcing. It also involves assigning them appropriate jobs. We will take these topics in turn in the following paragraphs.

What is Human resource management?
It is "the basic mission of human resources will always be to acquire, develop, and retain talent; align the workforce with the business; and be an excellent contributor to the business. Those three challenges will never change."[4]

---

[4] Gubman, Edward L. "The Gauntlet is Down." *Journal of Business Strategy*. November-December 1996.

According to another source, "Human Resource Management is the term used to describe formal systems devised for the management of people within an organization. The responsibilities of a human resource manager fall into three major areas: <u>staffing</u>, <u>employee compensation and benefits</u>, and <u>defining/designing work</u>."5 Also "human resource management is concerned with hiring, motivating and maintaining workforce within businesses."6
We adopt these aspects for the purpose of this writing.

Staffing

The Prophet (ﷺ) has recruited from three sources: the first one was the companions and this means that the people who were living in Madinah and surrounding areas. The Prophet (ﷺ) has also sent a message to other tribes of the area i.e. the Arab tribes to join them for the expedition; he had also sent a message to the people of Makkah for the same purpose.

All these people responded very positively as soon as they received the information they started to come in Madinah. Within a few

---

5https://www.inc.com/encyclopedia/human-resource-management.html
6https://medium.com/@swaticbindia/human-resource-management-its-core-functions-managerial-operative-fc0335ef616a

weeks, many people gathered in the city, one biographer has said that the number was up to 30000. Mubarikpuri says,

> No sooner had the Muslims heard the voice of the Messenger of Allâh (peace be upon him) calling them to fight the Byzantines than they rushed to comply with his orders. With great speed, they started getting ready for war. Tribes and phratries from here and there began pouring in Madinah. All the Muslims responded positively.[7]

So, the Prophet (ﷺ) ordered to prepare a register for them; all the names had been recorded. The purpose was to define a management strategy. The first part of the strategy was to organise these people in small groups or in manageable groups. Traditionally each tribe was headed by its chief, therefore, the Prophet (ﷺ) had organised all the tribes under the command of their chiefs. We understand there were two big tribes in Medina: Aus and Khizraj. They were being headed by their respective chiefs. According to his noble habit he had appointed Mohammed bin Musalma (RA) as the head of Madinah and appointed Ali (RA) to look after his family. The hypocrites objected but the Prophet (ﷺ) said that he was functioning like Haroon (AS) did for Musa (AS). Ali (RA) was happy and other people accepted his decision.

---

[7] P. 583.

Resourcing/compensation and benefits
It was the responsibility of the state to provide resources to potential military personnel so that they could participate in the battle. Nevertheless, enough transport was not available, therefore, many willing to join the expedition were returned. Mobarikpuri reports,

> "Even the needy and the poor who could not afford a ride came to the Messenger of Allâh (peace be upon him) asking for one so that they would be able to share in the fight against the Byzantines. But when he said:
>
> "... 'I can find no mounts for you' they turned back while their eyes overflowing with tears of grief that they could not find anything to spend (for Jihad)." [Surah At-Taubah:92][8]

Since there was a lack of resources, therefore, he has allocated 18 people to ride on a single camel. The camels also provided the food. They were used for meat as well as water they store in your body. When the Prophet (ﷺ) was passing through the distracted places of Saleh (AS) he asked people to drink water from the well from where the she-camel of Saleh (AS) was drinking the water. Further down to the destination the water was needed; he made a supplication to Allah (SWT) who sent down the rain. Similarly, when the Islamic troops reached Tabuk there was no water but there

---

[8] P. 583.

was a dry well, the Prophet (ﷺ) had made supplication again and the well filled with water for the people. They stayed 20 days over there and utilised the water of the well.

The Prophet (ﷺ) motivated his companions continuously; he was telling them glad tiding of paradise. He sent many a small battalion to various places against the local leaders and representatives of the Roman king especially those who were under the direct influence of him. Many of them agreed to pay tax to the Islamic government; it created incredibly positive impacts on the minds of people and the companions of the Prophet (ﷺ) as well. It was the motivation strategy which worked well.

The Prophet (ﷺ) used to distribute spoils of war among the participants which was considered a material benefit to the army but there was no war and no booty to distribute among the troops on this occasion. We understand that people were working for the Prophet (ﷺ) for the pleasure of Allah (SWT) without hoping any monetary compensation.

Defining/designing work
In terms of a battle, it implies assigning work to the leaders of the regiments. Lings describes the assignment of duties at the prominent level. He states "Hitherto it had been his practice not to divulge his true

objective at first, and to keep preparations as secret as possible. But this time there was no attempt at secrecy, and orders were sent to Mecca and to the allied tribes that they must send at once to Medina all their available armed and mounted men for the Syrian campaign."[9] The address was to the leaders of tribes so that they can collect their army and dispatch to the capital. Thus, the work was assigned to the heads of people. At individual level, he asked people to contribute money, food stuff, and animals.[10] Cash could be used for buying weapons, food was required for feeding the army in the journey; animals were used for mounting and food etc. He also urged everyone to participate in the battle to discharge religious responsibilities.

He also appointed a governor of Madinah, Ali (RA) was asked to stay behind to look after his family. According to Siddiqi the Prophet (ﷺ) had divided the army into groups/battalions, appointed commanders and flags were allocated.[11] The Prophet (ﷺ) had also allocated the number of people for mounting a camel. Eighteen soldiers were sharing a mount. There was sever scarcity of food and mounts but the army reached the destination with sacrifice.[12] While the Prophet (ﷺ) was in Tabuk, he sent

---

[9] P. 317.
[10] Mubarikpuri, p. 582-83.
[11] P. 505.
[12] Phalwarvi, p. 506.

Khalid bin Waleed (RA) to Dhomatul Jandhal who captured the leader of the area.[13] The man agreed to pay 'protection tax', thus became an ally of Muslims.

Motivation

Thang and his colleagues (2018) argue for the role of HRM which encompass motivation of employees so that they can work willingly and comfortably.[14] The Prophet (ﷺ) had motivated his companion at three occasions. The first time he inspired people was when he announced the expedition. He motivated people to fight in the path of Allah (SWT), a part of Surat Tobah was revealed for the inspiration of people. In addition, he described the virtues of spending for the cause of Allah (SWT) with money and efforts. Since it was a large army, it required motivation to strive in the path of Allah (SWT) And under the circumstances when the weather was hot, and people wanted to stay at home. They were suffering famine, and it was the time of harvesting the crops. They are mounting animals and there were few mounting animals because the journey was long. And the

---

[13] Shibli Noamani, p. 336-37.
[14] Thang Dang, Thai Tri Dung, Vu Thi Phuong, Tran Dinh Vinh, (2018) "Human resource management practices and firm outcomes: evidence from Vietnam", Journal of Asian Business and Economic Studies, Vol. 25 Issue: 2, pp.221-238.

travelling was difficult. The duration of the event was longer than the earlier such events.

The consequences of not doing this expedition were very grave. If the byzantine were to allow to enter in Medina and sent their troops near it. It would have long-term impacts on the reputation of Muslims. They could lose the goodwill they had earned so far. The Muslims understand that the earlier expeditions created positive impact on the minds of those tribes who were under the influence of the Byzantine empire. They started to support Muslims. It was one of the causes for the Byzantine to think about an invasion on Madinah. Because they wanted to end the danger forever as their ally Quraysh wished it for. But it was not child play.

The Prophet (ﷺ) had inspired his army again when he reached the destination. He described the goodness of this life and the Hereafter. Motivated towards eternal life. I warned against the punishment of Allah (SWT) and explained the rewards of Almighty. The purpose was to prepare people for the fight for which they travelled for two weeks. It was the right time to mentally reinforce the troops so that they could fight the enemy with zeal and enthusiasm. It has been the strategy of great leaders to infuse new power in the subordinates to achieve their goals. The Prophet (ﷺ) had applied the same strategy.

On the way back to Madinah new revelation came down to praise those who could not take part in the expedition due to unavailability of mounts. Quran 9:19.
On top of that, the Prophet (ﷺ) said near Madinah, there were some people in the city who were with you (in terms of rewards) while you were travelling in the desert. They were stopped due to acceptable excuses, so, they were equal to the travelers for Devine rewards. They earned the same pleasure of Allah (SWT) as you begged. However, there were three of them who could not join the expedition without an excuse. They were treated as such because they were true Muslims but could not took part due to human limitations. Allah (SWT) accepted their repentance.
It suggests that the Prophet (ﷺ) had motivated his subordinates before, during and after the event. In other words, motivation was a continuous activity which a manager must do daily.
The Prophet (ﷺ) had used the carrot and stick strategy. He described the rewards of Allah (SWT) and described the punishment of not making efforts in the path of Allah (SWT). He told about the people who could not take part in the battle but they received the same reward as the participants had received. Three of the companions who could not take part due to human limitations were reprimanded through social boycott which lasted for fifty days. Because the expedition was conducted for the

same period. The motivational strategy was a balanced approach, the subordinates accepted it and it worked very well. The success of the strategy is measured when it achieved its goals. The expedition had achieved its aims. The key goal of the expedition was according to Maulana Mubarakpuri[15] that the people of the Arab Peninsula started to understand that there is only one power in the area now and that was Islam. Therefore, the hopes of pagans and hypocrites died out. Their last hope was with Byzantine Empire. They believed that the Byzantine could save the Arab Peninsula from the Muslims influence, but this expedition ended their hopes. They have accepted the Muslim influence.

Secondly, it was not necessary to be lenient with hypocrites, so Allah (SWT) has ordered to deal with them punitively. For example, it was not allowed to take part in the funeral of hypocrites, not to accept their charity, do not to supplicate for them and visit their graves. The mosque they had constructed was demolished. The new revelation showed their signs. So, it was not difficult for Muslims to recognize them; in other words, they were exposed to everyone now. Finally, the expedition forced other tribes of the region to accept Islam so, many tribes visited Madinah and took the shelter under the shadow of Islam. Islam spread in the Arab peninsula after this event and the Muslim government

---

[15] P. 590-91.

set up in the region i.e., extended its boundaries to the areas whose leaders agreed to pay tax.

Managing discipline
Since the expedition was a special event under the circumstances of hardship yet it created three groups; one of them were the true Muslims, the second was hypocrite and the third was good Muslims but could not participate in the event. Maulana Mubarakpuri writes that all true Muslims were with the Prophet (ﷺ). If somebody was not present the companion used to speak about it the Prophet (ﷺ) replied that if he would join you then it's good for you and if is not then Allah (SWT) saved you from his mischief/harm.[16] It implies that the Prophet (ﷺ) had not pressurized anyone for joining the event. However, the mutual understanding about non-participants was negative except the true Muslims.

The results of the expedition were bad for the hypocrites because they do not take part openly in the event it means that they are open. Therefore, a decisive action was needed against them, so the Prophet (ﷺ) had demolished the mosque they had constructed for meeting and conspiring against Muslims.

---

[16] P. 588.

There were three persons who were good Muslims but could not take part in the expedition. The Prophet (ﷺ) had resolved their matter as per the guidance of Almighty. He announced a social boycott with them; no one was allowed to talk with them for 40 days, and thereafter they were asked to get separate from their wives. At last, the forgiveness was revealed, and their difficulty came to an end. And they joined the community as usual. It was with the permission of Almighty.

So, we can conclude that is those who could not participate due to lack of resources where appreciated. The hypocrites were punished and the true Muslims were reprimanded. It suggests that the Prophet (ﷺ) had applied both the stick and the carrot strategy to manage the disciplinary issues.

3 FINANCIAL MANAGEMENT

Introduction

The purpose of the chapter is to discuss fiscal management. Since many people supposed to be financed yet the Prophet (ﷺ) had raised finance to inject it in the process of management. As we understand that the purpose of fiscal management is to raise finance, utilise it and keep in reserve if something is left behind.

In other words, fiscal management deals with acquisition, utilisation, and preservation of financial resources. In this chapter, we will investigate these aspects from the perspective of the expedition. The major source of finance was the donation contributed by companions. The utilisation of resources was on the troops; it includes working capital for food and other supplies during the journey. Some resources were used for acquisition of hardware. Since there was no battle and consequently there was no booty acquired by the Muslims, therefore, nothing was available to distribute among the troops. Therefore, financing the requirements of the troops was a key question in front of the Prophet (ﷺ). It may be worthwhile to mention that a Muslim employee/soldier/manger receive dual reward. One is tangible and the other is intangible, the reward of any investment of time or capabilities in the Hereafter. As we understand that there was no tangible reward, but intangible was promised.

What is fiscal management?
It has been defined as the "supervision and handling of the financial affairs of an organization."[17] It includes acquisition, application/utilisation, and preservation of financial resources of an organisation. There is another view of the concept, according to it "Financial Management means planning, organizing, directing, and controlling the financial activities such as procurement and utilization of funds of the enterprise. It means applying general management principles to financial resources of the enterprise."[18] We adopt the first definition because it is a simple one and a common person can understand it easily. The audiences of the book are the non-specialist which demands that common language should be used to explain basic concepts and theories.

---

[17]https://www.collinsdictionary.com/dictionary/english/financial-management
[18]https://www.managementstudyguide.com/financial-management.htm

Acquisition of resources

An Islamic government can generate resources/funds through donation, share of booty, protection tax from non-muslims and zakat. The major source of finance was donation in the campaign.

When the Prophet (ﷺ) decided to move to his destination, he requested for the contribution from the companions. The major contributors were Osman (RA) and Abdul Rahman bin Ouff (RA), Abu Bakr (RA) and Umar (RA). However, every Muslim contributed to their best. It has been reported that Usman (RA) contributed one-third of the total resources. He contributed 1000 horses and camels and a lot of money in cash. Abdul Rahman Ouff (RA) contributed more than 200 gold coins. Table 1 shows the details of all the major contributors. Despite the resources, there was a general scarcity of resources. People travelled with great sacrifice.

Table 1 Contribution of companions[19]	
Name	Contribution
Abu Bakr (RA)	4000 Dhirham in cash
Umer bin Khattab (RA)	Half of his belongings

---

[19] Mubarikpuri, p. 583-84.

Usman bin Affan (RA)	1000 dhinar, 200 Okia; 900 Camels and 100 horses
Abdurrehman bin Ouff (RA)	200 Okia
Asim bin Addi (RA)	13.5 Ton dates

Hazrat Abbass (RA), Hazrat Talhah (RA), Hazrat Saad bin Abadhah (RA), and Muhammad bin Masalmah (RA) also brought a lot of gear/stuff. At individual level, one companion had nothing to donate; he worked for someone and earned four measures of dry dates. He contributed half of it and the balance left for his family.[20] Women also contributed their jewellery. In addition, "orders were sent to Mecca and to the allied tribes that they must send at once to Medina all their available armed and mounted men for the Syrian campaign."[21]

Utilisation of resources
Most of the contributors contributed camels, horses for mounting and foodstuff for supplies on the way to the journey. The Prophet (ﷺ) had devoted all the animals for mounting the troops; one camel was allocated for 18 people. They were taking turns to mount the animal. Some camels were slaughtered for food and waters. The food stuff was consumed during

---

[20] Siddiqui, p. 505.
[21] Lings, p. 316.

the journey. Water was scare in the desert but available at various places. There was a small well in Tabuk; the Prophet (ﷺ) had taken some water and washed his hands and face and poured the water in the well. The well started to gush. All quenched their thirst of it. The well remained active for centuries. Some believe the well is still active.[22]

Reservation of resources
The donated animals had been slaughtered for food and the remaining world kept as reserve for the future use. There was a small financial department in Medina because the demand for money was greater than supply. There was np booty on this occasion which could be distributed. The contribution collected at the commencement of the battle supposed to be kept as reserve. However, there is little mention about it.

It is worthwhile to note that provision of mounts was the responsibility of the government as we have seen that there are many people who could not participate in this expedition because the mounts were not available to them. Therefore, they could not participate; Allah (SWT) exempted them from the duty.
There was no shortage of Weapons during this expedition because everyone was keeping his

---

[22] Shoqi, p. 431.

own weapons. Sometime the Prophet (ﷺ) had supplied weapons to the army. The above discussion suggests the Prophet (ﷺ) had generated financial resources and utilised them effectively and efficiently.

4 STRATEGIC MANGEMENT

Introduction

Strategic management deals with long-term plans and strategy. The expedition of Tabuk was conducted in response to the long-term threat of Byzantines. The impacts of the campaign were also far reaching as unfolded later. It suggests that some discussion should be made about strategic management.

Nature of strategic management?

"Strategic management is a management field focusing on long-term planning and the direction of the organization."[23] It involves planning, implementation, and evaluation of strategy.[24] Strategic management is concerned

---

[23]https://managementmania.com/en/strategic-management

[24]Muhammad Shujahat, Saddam Hussain, Sammar Javed, Muhammad Imran Malik, Ramayah Thurasamy, Junaid Ali, (2017) "Strategic management model with lens of knowledge management and competitive intelligence: A review approach", VINE Journal of Information and Knowledge Management Systems, Vol. 47 Issue: 1, pp.55-93,

with long term effects on the survival of organisation. The Prophet (ﷺ) has taken the first strategic decision when he conquered Makkah. Similarly, Hunain was another expedition which could be considered as a strategic move. Tabuk was important in this connection. We will try to find out the basic ingredients of the topic out of the case study.

Background

The second major strategic expedition was the Tabuk event. The purpose of this was to stop the enemy on the eastern side for an expected invasion on Madinah. In addition, another purpose of the expedition was to create influence upon the Arab tribes like Ghassan. Because they were under the influence of Byzantine government. And they were trying to make alliance with the Byzantine Empire. The Prophet (ﷺ) also wanted to stabilize the Islamic influence upon the tribes in the Arab Peninsula.

It had been reported that the Byzantine Empire was targeting the Muslims because it was the most powerful military machine of the time. As we have described that Sharjeel Ghassani killed the Muslim ambassador Haris Bin Umair (RA). In response to this, the Prophet (ﷺ) had sent a small army against

---

https://doi.org/10.1108/VJIKMS-06-2016-0035

Romans but they were not defeated completely. The Roman emperor was also feeling that the Arab tribes were receiving the Muslim influence because of this battle. He could not disregard these developments and he was also perceiving that Muslims were becoming a real danger for him. Because Muslims were slowly moving towards the boundary of Syria. It was a challenge for him. Therefore, he thought that the dangerous should be eliminated before it entered in his Empire. In addition, he thought that not doing a decisive action against Muslims could trigger disturbance in the Arab areas which were adjunct to his boundary line. Considering all these circumstances and issues he ordered the Ghassanies to get prepared for a focused action against the Muslims.

It implied for the Muslims that they had to take a long-term perspective to counter the problem. Consequently, the Prophet (ﷺ) had taken the decision to go out and challenge the enemy. We understand out of the management literature that strategic management involves formulation, implementation, and evaluation of strategy. It is done within the strategic intent.

Strategic intent
It includes vision, mission, defining business, and objectives.[25] The vision of the Prophet (ﷺ) was to convey the message of Allah (SWT) all over the world. The mission was to make it happen through peaceful means. The Prophet (ﷺ) sent an ambassador for the purpose as stated earlier. But Byzantine empire killed him. Consequently, the battle of Mota took place. The business definition the Byzantine government or its allies; customer function was an armed encounter, and the operation was manual.[26] The objective of Tabuk expedition was to defend the physical boundaries of the state. However, the armed encounter was opted as a last resort.

Planning the expedition
The Prophet (ﷺ) had made the strategy to encounter the enemy outside Madinah therefore, he travelled long distance to challenge the opponents. He had also tested the hypocrites and the true Muslims about their loyalties with the Prophet (ﷺ).

---

[25] https://sites.google.com/site/tribhuvansite/sm/sm102

[26] The business definition of an organization in terms of customer needs, customer groups and alternative technologies. The concept has been taken from https://sites.google.com/site/tribhuvansite/sm/sm102.

The Prophet (ﷺ) had formulated his Tabuk strategy accordingly. The purpose was to halt the enemy away from Madinah. It was possible through a powerful and courageous expedition. Consequently, he collected the largest consignment of his time. And travelled hundreds of miles away from the capital city.

He collected many resources including mounts and food supply. Kandhelvi (2012) reports the appeal for donation and response of the companions,

Rasulullaah (ﷺ) gave the Sahabah (RA) plenty of encouragement to fight in Jihaad and asked them to spend for the pleasure of Allaah. The Sahabah (RA) therefore donated most generously. The first to spend so generously was Hadhrat Abu Bakr (RA) who donated everything he owned, equalling four.
thousand Dirhams. Rasulullaah (ﷺ) asked him, "Have you left anything for your family?" he replied, "I have left Allaah and His Rasool (ﷺ) for them." Hadhrat Umar (RA) then arrived with half of his belongings. When Rasulullaah (ﷺ) asked him if he had left anything for his family, he replied, 'Yes, I have left half of what I have brought." (Another narration states that he had left as much as he had brought.) When Hadhrat Umar heard about what Hadhrat Abu Bakr (RA) had brought he said, "He has beaten me each time we have vied to do good."
Hadhrat Abbaas bin Abdil Muttalib (RA), Hadhrat Talha bin Ubaydillaah (RA), Hadhrat Sa'd bin Ubaadah (RA) and Hadhrat

Muhammad bin Maslama (RA) all donated large sums. Hadhrat Abdur Rahmaan bin Auf (RA) donated two hundred Awqiya of silver (equal to eight thousand Dirhams) while Hadhrat Aasim bin Adi (RA) contributed ninety Wasaq of dates. Hadhrat Uthmaan bin Affaan (RA) equipped a third of the army and in providing everything for a third of the army, he became the person who spent the most. In fact, he gave so much that it is said that he left them without any needs. The Sahabah (RA) report that Rasulullaah (ﷺ) then said, "Nothing that Uthmaan does after this can cause him any harm."

With great enthusiasm, the wealthy Sahabah (RA) spent in this worthy cause anticipating the rewards from Allaah. Those Sahabah (RA) who were less wealthy assisted those who were poorer than them. They would even bring their camels to one or two persons, asking them to ride in turns. Some people would even bring some money and give it to someone leaving on the expedition. In fact, even the ladies assisted those in every way they could. Hadhrat Ummu Sinaan Aslamiyya (RA) says that she saw a cloth spread out in front of Hadhrat Aa'isha (RA) in her room, which was filled with bangles, bracelets, anklets, earrings, rings, and other jewellery that the women had sent to assist the Muslim army in its preparations. The Muslims were suffering poverty at that time and because it was a time when the fruit crops were ripe and shady areas were sought after. People, therefore, preferred to stay at home and disliked leaving.

The weapons were not a big matter because everyone had his own sword, arrows, and other things.

The announcement was made about the destination right from the inception of the programme. The purpose was to realise that the event was a tough campaign. The circumstances were hard for the participants because it was harvesting period, and the travelling conditions were difficult. However, the Prophet (ﷺ) had motivated his followers who were already willing to fight for the cause of Allah (SWT).

Implementation

The strategy was implemented prudently. The Prophet (ﷺ) travelled to the destination and waited for 20 days for the enemy. But the opponents could not dare to face the Muslims. According to Mubarikpuri "Upon learning of the Muslims' march, the Byzantines and their allies were so terrified that none of them dared set out to fight. On the contrary, they scattered inside their territory."[27] It implied that enemy had accepted defeat. The Prophet (ﷺ) had sent small battalions for nearby areas to take them under his control. In the words of Mubarikpuri,

---

[27] P. 586.

The Head of Ailah, Yahna bin Rawbah came to the Messenger of Allâh (peace be upon him), made peace with him and paid him the tribute (Al-Jizya). Both of Jarba' and Adhruh peoples paid him tribute, as well. So, the Messenger of Allâh (peace be upon him) gave each a guaranteed letter, like Yahna's, in which he says:

l "In the Name of Allâh, the Most Beneficent, the Most Merciful. This is a guarantee of protection from Allâh and Muhammad the Prophet (ﷺ), the Messenger of Allâh, to Yahna bin Rawbah and the people of Ailah; their ships, their caravans on land and sea shall have the custody of Allâh and the Prophet (ﷺ) Muhammad, he and whosoever are with him of Ash-Sham people and those of the sea. Whosoever contravenes this treaty, his wealth shall not save him; it shall be the fair prize of him that takes it. Now it should not be lawful to hinder the men from any springs which they have been in the habit of frequenting, nor from any journeys they desire to make, whether by sea or by land."

The Messenger of Allâh (peace be upon him) dispatched Khalid bin Al-Waleed at the head of four hundred and fifty horsemen to 'Ukaidir Dumat Al-Jandal and said to him: "You will see him hunting oryxes." So, when Khalid drew near his castle and was as far as an eye-sight range, he saw the oryxes coming out rubbing their horns against the castle gate. As it was a moony night Khalid could see Ukaidir come out to hunt them, so he captured him — though he was surrounded by his men — and brought him back to the Messenger of Allâh (peace be upon him), who spared his life and made peace with him for the payment of two thousand camels, eight hundred heads of cattle, four hundred armours and four hundred lances. He obliged him to recognize the duty of paying tribute" [28]

A similar truce was drawn with him as the tribes of Dumat, Tabuk, Ailah, and Taima agreed. As a result, the Muslim Army returned to Madinah.

Two special incidents happened on the way to the destination. The first one was that when the Muslim Army was travelling through the remains of the nation of Saleh (AS); the Prophet (ﷺ) directed everyone to pass through the place quickly. However, they can drink water from the well from where the she-camel of Saleh (AS) used to drink. On the way back, some hypocrites tried to harm the Prophet (ﷺ) but failed.

He had taken another long-term decision when he demolished the mosque constructed by the hypocrites, therefore, a centre of conspiracy was destroyed.

---

[28] P. 586-87.

Evaluation
"Evaluation is the process of determining merit, worth, or significance; an evaluation is a product of that process" (Scriven, 1991, p. 53)[29] Maulana Mobarikpuri recaps the outcome of the expedition,

> The effect of this expedition was great as regards extending and confirming the Muslims' influence and domination on the Arabian Peninsula. It was obvious to everybody that no power, but Islam's would live long among the Arabs. The remainders of Jahiliya and hypocrites — who used to conspire steadily against the Muslims and who perpetually relied on Byzantine power when they needed support or help — these people lost their expectations and desires of ever reclaiming their ex-influence. Realizing that there was no way out and that they were to submit to the *fait accompli* (done deal), they gave up their attempts.
>
> From that time on, the Muslims no longer leniently or even gently treated hypocrites. Allâh not only bade Muslims to treat them severely, but He also forbade them to take their gift charities or perform prayer on their dead or ask Allah's forgiveness for them or even visit their tombs. Allâh bade the Muslims

---

[29] Scriven, M. (1991). Evaluation thesaurus. Fourth edition. Newbury Park: Sage. From https://www.futurelearn.com/courses/enhancing-learning-and-teaching/0/steps/26447

to demolish the mosque, which they verily appointed and used as a hiding place where they might practise their plots, conspiracy, and deceit. Some Qur'anic verses were sent down disclosing them publicly and utterly so that everybody in Madinah got to know their reality.

The significant impact that this invasion produced could be perceived in of the vast number of delegations who came successively to meet the Messenger of Allâh (peace be upon him). Naturally, deputations used to come to meet him at the end of an invasion particularly after Makkah Conquest but they were not as many as these nor were they as frequent as they were then in the wake of Tabuk event. It was certainly the greatest.[30]

In short, the expedition achieved its strategic objectives, to create long-term influence of Muslims on the enemy, their allies, and others. These parties embraced the superiority of Islam. The geographical boundaries of the new Islamic state were extended. A new stream of revenue was generated to finance the affairs of the state. Thus, the door of success opened to the new religion.

---

[30] P. 590-91. Some corrections were made in the original translation.

5 INFORMATION MANAGEMENT

Introduction
Information management is important for any organisation because managers can make informed decisions based upon right and timely input. Tabuk was a military project which depends on the timing and quality of information. The awareness of enemy intentions, preparation and strength are vital for formulation of effective strategy. This chapter is reserved to know the information strategy of the Prophet (ﷺ).

Information management
Association of Project Management (APM) defines information management (IM) as "information management is the collection, storage, dissemination, archiving and destruction of information. It enables teams and stakeholders to use their time, resource and expertise effectively to make decisions

and to fulfil their roles."³¹ It involves gathering and conveying of accurate information on time.

The Prophet (ﷺ) had developed a network of gathering and communicating information in connection with the expedition. The network of the Prophet (ﷺ) was formal as well as informal. The formal network was based upon its own people while the informal systems depended upon the traders and other people. For example, the traders of oil informed that Hercules had collected an army of 40,000 people including the Arab troops. The army was under the leadership of a great commander of Room. They had sent an advanced party to Belqa. Consequently, the Prophet (ﷺ) had ordered the army to assemble in Madinah including confederate Arabs and people from Makkah.

The written record was maintained to enter the names of all the participants. Similarly, all the donations were also recorded as we have described in one of the tables in the earlier chapters. The purpose was to keep the record of all people and the donations. In addition, information was also kept in mind (tacit knowledge) about those who did not participate including the true Muslims about which we have discussed in the previous

---

[31] https://www.apm.org.uk/body-of-knowledge/delivery/integrative-management/information-management/

chapters. An informal record of hypocrites was also kept. It was the basis of actions taken against non-participants and the hypocrites. When limited resources were distributed to the substantial number of troops, calculation was made about how many people can ride an animal. It has been reported that eighteen people were sharing one camel.

Written communication

The Prophet (ﷺ) also use treaties in black and White with many heads of States including the people of Eelah, Jerbah, and Azruh. The text of the truce was,

"In the Name of Allâh, the Most Beneficent, the Most Merciful.

This is a guarantee of protection from Allâh and Muhammad the Prophet (ﷺ), the Messenger of Allâh, to Yahna bin Rawbah and the people of Ailah; their ships, their caravans on land and sea shall have the custody of Allâh and the Prophet (ﷺ) Muhammad, he and whosoever are with him of Ash-Sham people and those of the sea. Whosoever contravenes this treaty, his wealth shall not save him; it shall be his fair prize that takes it. Now it should not be lawful to hinder the men from any springs which they have been in the habit of frequenting, nor from any journeys they want to make, whether by sea or by land."[32]

Statistics was also kept about the number of people. The counts were maintained for the total number of participants,[33] the small expedition sent under the command of Khalid Bin Waleed (RA) to the leader of Dhumatul Jandal, the number of troops with him was 420.[34] There were 4 true Muslims who could not participate.[35] The duration of the campaign was 50 days, the Islamic army stayed in Tabuk for 20 days. The number of hypocrites left behind was more than eighty.[36]

In connection with one of the peace pacts, the Prophet (ﷺ) had done with the leader of Dhomatul Jundhal. The account was kept for the booty they had collected from him. It includes two thousand Camels, eight hundred slave, four hundred shields and four hundred spears.

In addition, on the way back twelve hypocrites try to harm the Prophet (ﷺ). The cleaver eyes of the Prophet (ﷺ) where upon them and he knew their intentions, as a result, he sent Huzaifa Razi Allah Tala anhu to counter them.

---

[32] Mubarikpuri, p. 586-87.
[33] Shibli, total 30,000 including 10,000 horse riders, p. 336.
[34] Phalwarvi says they were 400 (p. 507).
[35] Lings, p. 319.
[36] Siddiqui, p. 506; Phalwarvi says they were approximately 82. (p. 506)

Allah (SWT) had created fear in their minds, and they could not dare to achieve their goals.

Dissemination of information

One purpose of information system is to send information to subordinates including managers so that they can make informed decisions. The Prophet (ﷺ) had informed the subordinates where to go before starting the journey. He had sent people to inform the forces of Arabs and people of Mecca to join him for the expedition. On the way to the Tabuk, Muslim army had to travel through the area of Saleh (AS). The Prophet (ﷺ) informed them that they travel fast from the area, but you can drink water from the well from where the she-camel of Saleh (AS) used to drink. When he reached the destination, he informed the companions that there would be a storm so be careful about it.

The Prophet (ﷺ) regularly informed those companions who could not participate in the expedition about the decision of Almighty. For instance, for up to 40 days there was social boycott with these people and afterwards, more severe decision was made. They were informed that they should also get separate from their wives. At the end, the good news was communicated to them that their punishments had finished, and their repentance had been accepted. It was announced openly through another companion. Therefore, everybody listened to the announcement. There was a smile on the faces of everyone on this occasion. It suggests that he has kept the flow of information systematically and in an efficient manner. It could be one of the reasons for the success of the expedition.

When the Prophet (ﷺ) reached the destination, he delivered a comprehensive lecture to motivate people for the expedition telling them the virtues of fighting in the cause of Allah (SWT) and the rewards Allah (SWT) has kept for those who strive in the path of Allah (SWT). He also described the punishment of Allah (SWT) for those who hesitate to spend their time and money in the path of Allah (SWT).

Key points

We understand that the Prophet (ﷺ) are sent to convey the message of Allah (SWT) to their nations. They receive the information from Him and send them to the masses. People used to memories and write Devine revelation. The companions had done the same; it helped Usman (RA) to compile the words of Almighty in the form of a book later. The second chapter of the holy book states in the beginning that this book is free of doubt.

The Prophet (ﷺ) had applied the same strategy to manage the expedition. In addition to other aspects, we can say that the Prophet (ﷺ) had managed information effectively and efficiently. The key points of his strategy were:

- Constantly kept informed the stakeholders.
- Applied formal and informal sources.
- Allah (SWT) used to inform him of hidden aspects such as the intentions of hypocrites.
- The written record was kept systematically.
- Humans were the primary source of collection and dissemination of information. The tacit knowledge was in the memories of people. It could be extracted/retrieved as and when needed.

Bibliography

Adair, John (2010) The Leadership of Muhammad (PBUH), New Delhi: Kogan Page India Private Limited.

Al-Bahaqi, Abi Bakker Ahmad Al-Hussain (2009) Dhalail Al-Nabuwwa, Karachi: Dharul Ishaat.

Allen, Louis A. (1958) Management and organization, New York: McGraw-Hill.

DeCenzo, David A. and Stephen P. Robbins (2010) Human Resource Management, New York: John Wiley & Sons.

Dess, Gregory G., G. T. Lumpkin, Alan B. Eisner (2006) Strategic Management: Text and Cases, New York: Irwin/McGraw-Hill.

Dyck, B and Mitchell J Neubert (2009) Principal of Management, South-Western.

Fulop, L, and S Linstead (1999) Management, A critical text, London: Macmillan.

Gilani, Mnazar Ahsan Gilani (1936) Al-Nabi Al-Khatam Sallallaho Alaihay Wasallam (Urdu), Jayyad Barqi Press: Dehli.

Gubman, Edward L. "The Gauntlet is Down." *Journal of Business Strategy*. November-December 1996.

Haimann, Theo and Raymond L. Hilgert (1972) Supervision: Concepts and Practices of Management, South-Western Publishing Company.

Hameed Ullah, M. (2006) The Prophet's (ﷺ) Establishing a State and his Succession, Beacon Books: Lahore.

Iqbal, Javed, and Muhammad Mushtaq Ahmad (2009) Planning in the Islamic Tradition: The Case of Hijrah Expedition, INSIGHTS 01(3), 37-68.

Kaandhlawi, Muhammad Zakarya (1997), Fazail-e-Amaal, Lahore: Kutibkhana Faizi.

Kaandhlawi, Muhammad Yusaf (2012), Hayatus Sahabah, Delhi: Islamic Books Services.

Koontz, Harold, and Heinz Weihrich (2006) Essentials of Management, New Delhi: Tata McGraw-Hill Education, pp. 81-84.

Kreitner, R (2009) Principal of Management, South-Western.

Lings, M (1994) Muhammad, his life based on the earliest sources, Lahore: Suhail Academy.

Mubarakpuri, Safiur Rahman (1995) "The Sealed Nectar" (Ar-Raheeq Al-Makhtum), Lahore: Al-Maktba Alsalfia.

Muhammad ibn Ishaq, (2004) The Life of Muhammad, Oxford University Press, Karachi.

[1]Muhammad Shujahat, Saddam Hussain, Sammar Javed, Muhammad Imran Malik, Ramayah Thurasamy, Junaid Ali, (2017) "Strategic management model with lens of knowledge management and competitive intelligence: A review approach", VINE Journal of Information and Knowledge Management Systems, Vol. 47 Issue: 1, pp.55-93.

Nadvi, Sulaiman Hussaini (2205) Khutbat-e-Seerat, Karachi: Zam-Zam Publishers.

Noamani, Shibli and Syed Solaiman Nadhvi (2004) Seeratun-Nabi, Karachi: Dharul-Ishaat.

Pea, Roy D. (2015) What Is Planning Development the Development of? Accessed: April 2015, http://web.stanford.edu/~roypea/RoyPDF%20folder/A11_Pea_82d.pdf

Phalwari, Muhammad Jaafer (1995) Peghambr-e-Insaniat, Lahore: Idara Sakafat-e-Islamia.

Razi, Muhammad Wali (1987) Hadhi-e-Alam, Dharul-Ilm: Karachi.

Robbins, Stephen, and Mary Coulter (2017) Management, New Delhi: Pearson Education.

Saani, Javed Iqbal (2017) Prophet (ﷺ) Muhammad (ﷺ) as a planning expert, London: Intellectual Capital Enterprise Limited.

Saani, Javed Iqbal (2016) Responsibilities of Managers: Selected Ahadith, available on amazon.co.uk. (Paperback edition)

Scriven, M. (1991). Evaluation thesaurus. Fourth edition. Newbury Park: Sage.

Shoqi, Abu Khalil (2002) Atlas-Seerat-e-Nabvi, Darussalam: Lahore.

Siddiqi, Naeem (1997) The Benefactor of Humanity (Mohsin-e-Insaniyat), Dehli: Markazi Matabah Islami Publishers.

Smith, Mike (2007) Fundamentals of Management, Berkshire: McGraw Hill Education.

Time Management Guide (2015) What is planning and why you need to plan, Accessed: April 2015, http://www.time-management-guide.com/planning.html

Thang Dang, Thai Tri Dung, Vu Thi Phuong, Tran Dinh Vinh, (2018) "Human resource management practices and firm outcomes: evidence from Vietnam", Journal of Asian Business and

Books of Ahadith

Imam Muhammad ibn Isma`il al-Bukhari al-Ju`fi (1983) Sahih Al-Bukhari, Translated by Muhammad Muhsin Khan, Lahore: Kazi Publications.

Imâm Abut Hussain Muslim bin al-Hajjaj, SahIh Muslim, Translated by Nasiruddin al-Khattab, Riyadh, 2007, Maktaba Dar-us-Salam.

Imam Muslim ibn al-Ḥajjaj̄ al-Qushayrī (1971-75) Translated by Abdul Hameed Siddiqui Sahih Muslim, Lahore, Sh. Muhammad Ashraf.

lmâm Hâfiz Abu Dawud, Sunan Abu Dawud Sulaiman bin Ash'ath, Maktaba Dar-us-Salam, Riyadh, 2007.

Imäm Hãfiz Abü 'Elsa Mohammad Ibn 'Elsa At-Tirmidhi, Jamia' At-Tirmıdhi, English Translation by Abu Khaliyl, Riyadh, 2007, Maktaba Dar-us-Salam.

Imiim Hiifiz Abu Abdur Rahmiin Ahmad bin Shu'aib bin 'Ali An-Nasa'i, Sunan An-Nasa'i, Riyadh, 2007, Maktaba Dar-us-Salam.

Imam Muhammad Bin Yazeed Ibn Majah Al-Qazwinf, Sunan Ibn Majah Translated by Nasiruddin al-Khattab, Riyadh, 2007, Maktaba Dar-us-Salam.

Abu Zakaria Al-Nawawi, Riyad-us-Saliheen, Riyadh, 2007, Maktaba Dar-us-Salam.

Imam Malik bin Ans (رضي الله عنه), Muwatta Imam Malik, translated in Urdu by Allama Molana Abdul Hakeem Akhtar Shahjahanpuri, Lahore: Fareed Book Stall, accessed on 14 November 2017, https://readingpk.com/muwatta-imam-malik-imam-muhammad-malik/

https://www.sunnah.com

Index

A

Abbass (RA), 6, 26
Abdurrehman Bin Ouff (RA), 6, 26
Abu Bakr (RA), 6, 26, 35, 36
Ali (RA), 5, 12, 15
Allah, Xv
Allah (SWT), Xv, Xvii, 6, 13, 14, 18, 29, 51, 52
Anas, Vii
Animal, 27, 47
Arab, 3, 4, 5, 8, 11, 19, 32, 33, 46
Asim Bin Addi (RA), 6, 26
Association Of Project Management, 45

B

Battalion, 14
Battle, Xvii, 2, 3, 8, 12, 15, 19, 24, 28, 33, 34
Book, Ii, V, Xvii, 25, 52, 67
Books, 69
Business, Xviii, 9, 34
Byzantine, 3, 17, 19, 32, 34, 41

C

Camel, 13, 16, 27, 40, 47, 50
Campaign, 4, 5, 6, 15, 27, 31, 37, 49
Capital, 1, 15, 23, 35
Case Study, 69
Change, 69
Companions, Xvii, 6, 10, 14, 19, 23, 25, 26, 35, 50, 51
Compensation, 10, 12, 14

Consult, Ix
Contributors, 6, 25, 27

D

Donation, 23, 35

E

Effectively, 1, 29, 46, 52
Efficiently, 1, 29, 52
Empire, 3, 19, 32
Energy, 1
Evaluation, 31, 33, 41
Expedition, Xviii, 2, 6, 7, 9, 11, 12, 17, 18, 20, 21, 23, 28, 31, 32, 34, 35, 37, 41, 43, 46, 48, 50, 51, 52

F

Fazail-E-Amaal, X, 54
Financial Management, 23
Formal Network, 46

H

Hijrah, I, 54
HRM, 1, 9, 16
Human Resource Management, 1, 10
Hunain, 2, 32
Hypocrites, 4, 5, 12, 19, 21, 22, 35, 40, 41, 42, 47, 49, 52

I

Implementation, Xvii, 31, 33
Informal Systems, 46

Information, Xv, Xviii, 1, 11, 45, 46, 49, 51, 52
Information Management, Xviii
Iqbal, **Xix**
Islamic, V, 13, 14, 32, 49, 54

J

Journey, Xviii, 5, 7, 15, 17, 24, 27, 50

K

Kandhelvi, 35
Khalidh Bin Waleedh (RA), 7

L

Labour, 1
Land, 1, 39, 48
Leader, Ix, X, Xi
Lings, 6, 15, 27, 49, 54

M

Madinah, Xvii, 3, 4, 5, 6, 7, 10, 11, 12, 15, 17, 18, 32, 35, 40, 42, 46
Makkah, 2, 5, 6, 11, 32, 42, 46
Management, V, Xvii, 2, 9, 10, 11, 16, 23, 24, 25, 31, 33, 45, 46, 53, 54, 55, 56, 68
Manager, Ix, X, Xi, 1, 10, 19
Managers, 1, 45, 49
68, 69
Managing Discipline, 20
Manpower, 5
Materials, 1
Medina, 5, 12, 15, 17, 27, 28
Mission, 9, 34
Mosque, 20, 21, 40, 42
Motivating, 9, 10
Motivation, 16

Mubarikpuri, 3, 11, 15, 26, 38, 48
Muhammad, Vi, Ix, 53, 54, 55, 56, 57, 67, 68
Muhammad Bin Musalmah (RA), 6
Muslim, 2, 4, 8, 20, 24, 26, 33, 37, 40, 50, 57
Muslims, Xvii, 3, 4, 5, 7, 8, 11, 16, 17, 19, 20, 21, 24, 32, 33, 35, 37, 38, 41, 42, 43, 47, 48

N

Neubert (2009), 53

O

Objectives, Xvii, 18, 19, 34, 43, 49
Organization, V, 10, 24, 31, 34, 53

P

Participants, 2, 6, 14, 19, 21, 37, 47, 48
Phalwarvi, 16, 48, 49
Plan, 56
Planning, 4, 25, 31, 54, 56, 67
Production, 1
Productivity, 1, 2
Project, Xv
Prophet (ﷺ), Viii, Xvii, 1, 2, 4, 5, 6, 7, 8, 10, 11, 13, 14, 16, 18, 21, 22, 23, 24, 25, 27, 29, 32, 33, 34, 35, 37, 38, 39, 40, 45, 46, 47, 48, 49, 50, 51, 52, 56, 66, 67

Q

Quality, Xviii, 2, 45

R

Rasulullaah (ﷺ), X, 35, 36
Resources, Xviii, 1, 5, 6, 9, 12, 13, 22, 23, 24, 25, 26, 27, 28, 29, 35, 47
Resourcing, 9
Risk, 68
Romans, 2, 3, 4, 7, 8, 33

S

Saad Bin Ubaidhah (RA), 6
Scarcity, 16, 26
Selection, 9
Shibli, 16, 48, 55
Shoqi, 56
Siddiqi, Naeem, 16, 56
Stakeholders, 46, 52
Statistics, 48
Strategic Management, Xvii, 9, 31
Strategy, 11, 14, 18, 19, 22, 31, 33, 35, 38, 45, 52
Syria, 33

T

Tabuk, I, Xvii, 13, 16, 27, 31, 32, 34, 35, 40, 42, 45, 49, 50
Tacit Knowledge, 47, 52
Talha (RA), 6
Tribes, 3, 5, 6, 8, 11, 12, 15, 17, 20, 27, 32, 33, 40

U

Umer (RA), 6
Usman (RA), 6, 26, 51

V

Vision, 34

W

Weapons, 15, 29, 37
Written Communication, 47
Written Record, 46, 52

Other books by the author (s)

1. Prof Dr. Javed Iqbal Saani (2018) Managerial Implications of the Hijrah Expedition, Intellectual Capital Enterprise Limited, London, available on Amazon (Paperback edition)
2. Prof Dr. Javed Iqbal Saani (2018) Managerial Implications of the Battle of BADR, Intellectual Capital Enterprise Limited, London, available on Amazon (Paperback edition)
3. Prof Dr. Javed Iqbal Saani (2018) Managerial Thoughts of the Prophet (ﷺ), Intellectual Capital Enterprise Limited, London, available on Amazon (Paperback edition)
4. Prof Dr. Javed Iqbal Saani (2018) Controlling Strategy of the Prophet (ﷺ), Intellectual Capital Enterprise Limited, London, available on Amazon (Paperback edition)
5. Prof Dr. Javed Iqbal Saani (2018) Leading Strategy of the Prophet (ﷺ), Intellectual Capital Enterprise Limited, London, available on Amazon (Paperback edition)
6. Prof Dr. Javed Iqbal Saani (2018) Organising Strategy of the Prophet (ﷺ), Intellectual Capital Enterprise Limited, London, available on Amazon (Paperback edition)
7. Prof Dr. Javed Iqbal Saani (2018) Planning Strategy of the Prophet (ﷺ), Intellectual

Capital Enterprise Limited, London, available on Amazon (Paperback edition)
8. Prof Dr. Javed Iqbal Saani (2018) Qualities of Momins: The Quranic Perspective, Intellectual Capital Enterprise Limited, London, available on Amazon (Paperback edition)
9. Prof Dr. Javed Iqbal Saani (2018) Hajj Experience: Combining Dawah and Manasiks, Intellectual Capital Enterprise Limited, London, available on Amazon (Paperback edition)
10. Prof Dr. Javed Iqbal Saani (2018) Sukhn-e-Saani (The book of poetry), Intellectual Capital Enterprise Limited, London, available on Amazon (Paperback edition)
11. Prof Dr. Javed Iqbal Saani (2018) Managing Your Projects, Intellectual Capital Enterprise Limited, London, available on amazon.co.uk. (Paperback edition)
12. Prof Dr. Javed Iqbal Saani (2017) Business Case Studies, Intellectual Capital Enterprise Limited, London, available on Amazon (Paperback edition)
13. Prof Dr. Javed Iqbal Saani (2017) Virtues of Sickness: Selected Ahadith, available on Amazon (Paperback edition)
14. Prof Dr. Javed Iqbal Saani (2017) Prophet (ﷺ) Muhammad (ﷺ) as a planning expert, available on Amazon (Paperback edition)

15. Prof Dr. Javed Iqbal Saani (2017) Muhammad (ﷺ): His Trials & Tribulations, available on Amazon (Paperback edition)
16. Prof Dr. Javed Iqbal Saani (2017) Sales and Marketing: Selected Ahadith, available on amazon.co.uk. (Paperback edition)
17. Prof Dr. Prof Dr. Javed Iqbal Saani (2016) Research Proposals: Contents & Exemplars, available on amazon.co.uk. (Paperback edition)
18. Prof Dr. Javed Iqbal Saani (2016) Responsibilities of Managers: Selected Ahadith, available on amazon.co.uk. (Paperback edition)
19. Prof Dr. Javed Iqbal Saani (2016) Experience: The Journey of My Life, available on amazon.co.uk. (Paperback edition)
20. Prof Dr. Javed Iqbal Saani (2012) Understanding Information Systems, Manchester: GRaASS.
21. Prof Dr Javed Iqbal Saani (2011) Digital Divide in South Asia ISBN: 9789699578120.
22. Prof Dr. Javed Iqbal Saani and Muhammad Rafi Khattak (2011) Managing Risk in Projects, ISBN: 9789699578090.
23. Prof Dr. Javed Iqbal Saani and Muhammad Nadeem Khan (2011, 2018) Understanding Project Management, ISBN: 978969957845, available on Amazon (Paperback edition)

24. Prof Dr. Javed Iqbal Saani (2011) Information Systems for Managers, Grass Books, Manchester.
25. Prof Dr. Javed Iqbal Saani (2010) Managing strategic change: a real-world case study, ISBN: 978-3838330952, available on amazon.co.uk. (Paperback edition)

[Please see the images of these books on the following pages in addition to my doctoral thesis]

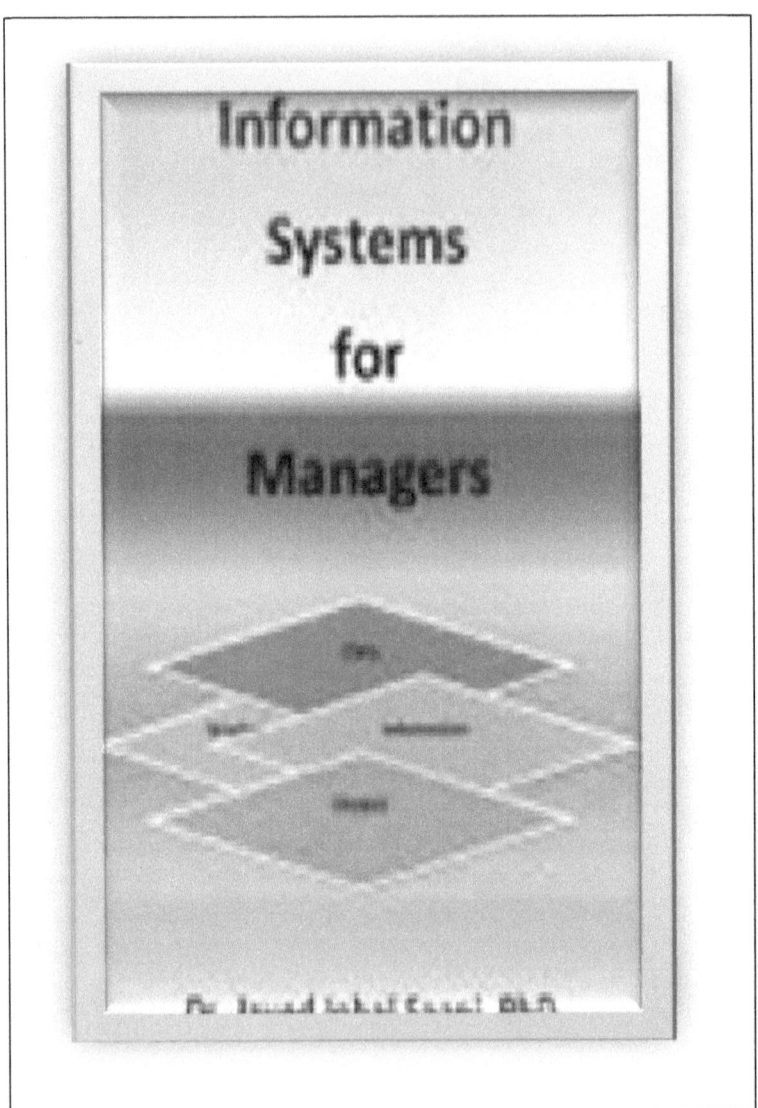

Notes